# INVESTMENT IN CRYPTO CURRENCY FOR BEGINNERS

Short Guide to Small Investments and Trade to Create Passive

**Eugene Black**

Text Copyright © Eugene Black

All rights reserved. No part of this guide may be reproduced in any form without permission in writing from the publisher except in the case of brief quotations embodied in critical articles or reviews.

ISBN-13: 978-1725959163

ISBN-10: 172595916X

**Legal & Disclaimer**

The content and information in this book has been provided for educational purposes only.

The content and information contained in this book has been compiled from sources deemed reliable, and it is accurate to the best of the Author's knowledge, information and belief. However, the Author cannot guarantee its accuracy and validity and cannot be held liable for any errors and/or omissions.

Upon using the contents and information contained in this book, you agree to hold harmless the Author from and against any damages, costs, and expenses, including any legal fees potentially resulting from the application of any of the information provided by this book.

You agree to accept all risks of using the information presented inside this book.

You agree that by continuing to read this book, where appropriate and/or necessary, you shall consult a professional.

# TABLE OF CONTENTS

INTRODUCTION ..................................................... 4

CHAPTER 1: Rock, Scissors, Paper ..................... 5

CHAPTER 2: To Be Or Not To Be?! ................... 9

CHAPTER 3: How To Earn? ............................... 11

CHAPTER 4: Stock Exchange ........................... 15

CHAPTER 5: How To Conquer Binance .......... 19

CHAPTER 6: First Binance Trade Steps ........ 33

CHAPTER 7: The Most Important ................... 44

CONCLUSION ...................................................... 46

# INTRODUCTION

Today, "bitcoin" and "crypto-currency" are words known by almost everyone. Of course, there are still a lot of people unfamiliar with how the cryptocurrency system works; therefore, it is not trusted. Nevertheless, an incredible growth of bitcoin led to high interest in the topic at the end of 2017. There was a real agiotage about the crypt. However, then followed the collapse and disappointment. The capitalization of cryptocurrency first increased abruptly, and then declined; the confidence and interest of the issue faded. Those who were interested in cryptocurrency made investments based on emotions during bitcoins' growth, certainly experienced deep disappointment, and perhaps, do not want to hear anything else about cryptocurrency again.

Let us sort out this subject a little more in order to have a calmer opinion of the world's digital currencies and avoid unnecessary emotions and speculations toward it. We will discuss this issue in general terms, without digging as deeply as some would like, yet enough to understand how to deal with cryptocurrency.

# CHAPTER 1
# Rock, Scissors, Paper

You, dear reader, probably know the game "Rock, Paper, Scissors," a game of rather simple rules, mostly used as a method of ballot. Our choice of any monetary system is most likely based on established traditions. We think rarely about the actual state of things; therefore, everything new and incomprehensible frightens us.

In this chapter, I suggest considering the difference between commodity money, fiat currency, and digital ones. It is for you to decide, my reader, which of them is better or worse.

## Commodity Money

A goods/money relationship will exist as long as there is a civilization. People always exchanged one product for another. Occasionally, some of the more general purpose type goods were used as money. Such goods have always been valued; they were easily calculated, accumulated, and transferred. Thus, this type of money had its certain value since it always remained as goods.

The simplest example of such commodity money is gold and silver. Today, there are not many civilizations and empires; nonetheless, minted silver and gold coins are still valued, even as precious metals.

The economy has always experienced recessions. During such times, even precious metals were losing their value. In periods like these, the state tries to launch a regulatory mechanism. These sorts of attempts have been made for several centuries by many governors, and as a result, the fiat money has appeared.

## Fiat and Fiduciary Money

The fiat money name came from the lat. fiat—a decree, an indication. It is about symbolic money that is not backed by a physical commodity/good. The value guarantee is as the government "decrees," which regulates its emission and nominal value.

This term was first used in the USA in the nineteenth century, before the existence of the "gold standard." At that time, currencies were divided into two types: fiduciary (tradeable) and fiat. The first had use value, and the issuing banks pledged to reimburse the bearer of such money with gold or silver. The second had no security.

The idea of fiat money was first expressed by Plato. He believed that the state should issue money, which ran on its territory and obliged the population to use only such currency. The first attempt to implement the idea into practice belonged to the Roman Emperor Diocletian, who ordered his citizens to use solid coin minted in Rome only. The currency had failed, and the law was soon canceled.

In the 11th century, in China, the first paper fiat money was set. The Chinese nicknamed them as "flying money" because they were blown away by the wind. It's important to mention that at the beginning, Chinese paper money had some success. However, the eternal problem of this currency was that the government could print such money in any quantity because it did not need backed up by a commodity, so it literally had no value. Sooner or later, the moment came when fiat money became cheaper than some toilet paper.

Nevertheless, fiat entered our life. In the nineteenth century, almost all countries of the world converted to the fiduciary currency. And if, at the beginning of its existence, such currency was backed by gold or silver, then the so-called "gold standard" today is not supported by any of the world's fiat currencies.

Therefore, every ten to twenty years, any of such currency is crashing, flinging over the state with a wave of inflation.

## Digital Money

The first digital money has nothing to do with cryptocurrency. Due to the development of computers and the internet, many fiduciary currencies have acquired a digital analog. These are our bank cards. There is a certain amount of digital money on your bank card, which is backed by the same amount of fiat physical money.

The bank issuer guarantees the exchange of digital money into physical money. We continue discussing only fiat money; the nominal value and emission of which is determined by the government.

And thus, in 2008, in response to another economic crisis, bitcoin appeared. No one paid much attention to that news, until the cost of bitcoin reached values that could not be missed!

I won't bother you, my reader, with the technical explanations and details on what blockchain is. If you want, this information can be found on the internet. Let us confine ourselves with the fact that cryptocurrency technology is based on cryptography, which in itself, has been around for quite some time. Essentially, cryptocurrency also wasn't backed up by a commodity either. Nowadays, it is itself a commodity, and in contrast with fiat money, its nominal value and emission are not controlled by the state. The nominal value and emission of digital money depends on users of the worldwide internet network only! Just this unique fact makes the cryptocurrency so desirable and interesting for many!

## CHAPTER 2
# To Be Or Not To Be?!

One of the strongest questions ever for anyone who pays attention to cryptocurrency is perhaps it's just a soap-bubble that can burst at any time? In my opinion, there is no sense in moving forward without having an answer to that question. Therefore, my reader, let me offer my answer to you.

As mentioned before, the cost of cryptocoins (nowadays, there are about 1,500 different kinds of coins) is determined by users of the internet around the world. The advanced interest to a particular coin increases its value. Neither state in the world can control this process by laws and decrees. Similarly, the issue of new coins (their emission) also depends on users of the network and is determined by the program code of the specific coin. Once again, the state cannot influence this process in any way. Thus, the cryptocurrency will be around as long as the internet and interest for cryptocurrency exist.

Obviously, such independence of the cryptocoin's holders dissatisfies the government. It didn't bother anyone while being small and free. Today, politicians and bankers around the world are seriously concerned about the impact of the cryptocurrency on the world's financial system. Their real concern is what to do? There is neither a way to control all users of the worldwide internet nor is the government able to provide energy resources to create the cryptocurrency independently like fiat money. Another option is to destroy the cryptosystem itself by eliminating the internet first, which would be a real disaster!

The only option to concider is to join the process and try to lead it! While politicians and bankers are racking their brains on how to do it, almost every inhabitant of the planet who has access to the internet and a couple hundred dollars in his pocket can make money on cryptocurrency. In the following chapters, we will look at several options on how you can earn money and give some advice for beginners.

Completing this chapter, I would like to say that in order to get all the benefits from cryptocurrency, you don´t have to know the detailed technology of its release and turnover. Same with electricity, you don´t have to be an electrician and know the exact physics of the process in order to use electricity. It is enough to flick the switch to light up the room! In fact, it will light up even if you don´t believe in the power of electricity!

Nonetheless, if you are really interested in the physics of the cryptocurrency system, detailed information can be found in other publications or on the internet.

## CHAPTER 3
# How To Earn?

So, my friend, supposedly you´ve decided that the topic of cryptocurrency is interesting to you, and you would like to try your hand in it. Then, it is time to find the answer to the next question: how do you make money on the crypt? Let's briefly list the main types of earnings and then look into the details of some of them.

## Sale of Goods and Services for Bitcoins

Yes, yes, you already can pay with bitcoins. You will get the bitcoins, if they are ready to pay you with it. The received crypt can be saved or used for other types of earnings, as well as to be exchanged into fiat money. In any case, you´ll need a cryptocurrency wallet. Of course, the most reliable one is a paper one, but the web wallets are more convenient. When choosing a wallet, read reviews and opinions about it.

# Mining

Mining is the immediate extraction of bitcoin or some other type of cryptocoin. A special program should be installed on your computer in order to do it. The coins are mined by your computer. However, if earlier it could be done on your home PC, nowadays for mining, you will need more powerful equipment. Besides, the process itself consumes a lot of electricity, and in some countries, where electricity tariffs are high, it is not profitable to mine.

# Invest in Bitcoin Companies

This is the purchase of a bitcoin company's shares on an exchange market. Among them are Bitcoin Investment Trust, Bitcoin Shop, SmartMetric, and others. The advantage of such companies is that they are working not only in the cryptocurrency environment, but also in the world of fiat money.

# Bitcoin Cranes

The crane is a site that pays its users Satoshi (the smallest bits of bitcoin) for certain actions, for example, for watching some advertisements. Originally, the purpose of these sites was to promote the cryptocurrency; however, they are still popular.

This method doesn´t require any financial investments. There is no risk at all, but earnings are very small, too.

# Trading

You can start trading with a cryptocurrency on one of the exchanges if you have a certain amount of fiat money that you are willing to risk (more details on the exchange will be in the next chapter). There are several options for trading.

Buy the cryptocurrency on one exchange, and sell it on another. This kind of trade requires a lot of time, a lot of money, and experience to return the commission.

Also, you can trade within the same exchange market. The advantage of this method is the possibility to start trading with a very modest amount: $50-100. However, in order to get more or less valueble results, it is better to start with the amount of about $500. It is rather risky, like in any other business. We´ll talk about this method more in the future, but for now, let's talk about other ways of earning that are worthy of your attention.

## Portfolio Set Up and Storage of the Cryptocurrency

You buy several coins in different proportions on the exchange market and create a portfolio of your cryptocoins, then you should wait for the exchange rate to increase and sell them with a 30-70 percent profit. This is a very simplified scheme, but quite pleasing. First and foremost, we are talking about the long-term (from six to twelve months or more) storage of coins.

If this occurs, then you will also need a cryptocurrency wallet since it is not recommended to keep money on the exchange.

Participation in Mutual Funds and Initial Coin Offering (ICO) Investments

In the first case, in order to make a profit, you entrust your means to the cryptocurrency fund. In the second—you invest your money into a new, developing project. If the project is successful—you earn, if not, then you lose the invested funds. There are several other ways to earn the cryptocurrency, but they are either too risky (for example, gambling) or not worthy of consideration (different financial pyramids).

## CHAPTER 4
# Stock Exchange

Well, my dear reader! It's time to talk about exchange itself. I personally believe that cryptocurrency has enabled many to try their hand in trading stocks. Consider for yourself, this cryptocurrency is a rather new asset. It still lacks lots of complexities to which the stock and securities are exposed. You don't need an intermediary (exchange broker) to start trading because registration on your own is still available on many of them.

Cryptocurrency exchange appears every year, and some of them disappear (one of the reasons why you cannot keep your funds on the exchange). Nonetheless, if you decide to try your hand on it, in order to start, you should choose an exchange. It is unnecessary to register at once with several different exchanges. For the starters, one will do. A list of the top most popular and most reliable exchanges can always be found on the internet. I offer you a short list of exchanges, which are surely suitable for a beginner.

# EXMO

ww.exmo.com

The office of this exchange is in Great Britain. The advantage of this exchange is in the simplicity of the interface, a small commission, and good technical support. Besides bitcoin and other coins, the exchange trades with some fiat money, including USD and Euro. You can withdraw your earnings on any plastic card. The commission for any transaction is 0.02 percent.

# KuCoin

www.kucoin.com

This is the Hong Kong, actively growing cryptocurrency trade, launched in the middle of September 2017. The exchange operates quickly and is stable. It trades in many currency pairs, and has its own mobile application. There is 24/7 customer support provided. For small quantities, the mandatory verification is not required. The commission is 0.01 percent, and for some other coins, could be even 0% percent at all.

# Poloniex

www.poloniex.com

The Poloniex Exchange is one of the largest in the world. It was founded in 2014. The exchange offers the biggest number of currency pairs for trading.

The advantages: a simple interface, good analytical tools, and a cheap commission from 0 percent to 0.25 percent.

The disadvantages: a lack of a mobile application, slow work process (compared to other exchanges), and customer support works only through e-mail. Also, there is no fiat money on this exchange, so withdrawal of funds is possible only in the cryptocurrency.

Generally speaking, if you are a beginner, it won´t be difficult for you to understand this exchange.

## HitBTC.

www.hitbtc.com

The exchange was founded in 2013. It trades the most popular currency pairs in a large amount. This list is constantly replenished. Here, on HitBTC, you can trade with fiat money, too. This exchange was originally developed for users of different levels; therefore, the site is perfect for beginners to trading as well.

Unfortunately, there is a commission not only for transactions, but also for a deposit in bitcoin. Thus, if you have a small amount, it is better to start working with another exchange.

# Binance

www.binance.com

Binance is one of the youngest and most popular exchanges. The registration here is quite simple. There is a possibility to trade with a large amount of currency pairs. The low commission—0.01 percent. One of the biggest advantages of the exchange is its high productivity. Binance can handle about 1.4 million orders per second!

There is no fiat money on this exchange, but in 2018, it became the first in terms of trading volume. Its simplicity and popularity deserves our attention; therefore, in the future, we will focus more on it. We'll show you how to register, start and withdraw money, and also engage in trading on those exchanges using Binance as an example. My reader, it doesn't mean that you need to register on Binance only. The principles are considered applicable to any of the exchanges that were described above.

## CHAPTER 5
# How To Conquer Binance

Let's get started. The registration process on the Binance exchange is very simple and should not cause any difficulties. Fortunately, there aren't any restrictions for the registration of new users yet. Since January 2018, one of the most popular Bitfinex exchanges introduced a mandatory condition for registering an account; it was necessary to have a minimum of $10,000, or the EXMO, in order to start trading required mandatory verification.

Binance is still open for starters; the opportunity shoudn't be wasted. However, the registration for new users becomes unavailable from time to time. Most likely, it is due to technical maintenance of the site. But anyway, it is still possible to register by using an affiliate link. This link can be found at the end of this chapter.

First, you should type in the search box of the browser "Binance," and go to the trading platform. Also, you can type binance.com in the address box or insert a referral link into it. (Pic. 1)

As an advantage of this exchange, you can use its tools, view graphics, stockware, etc., except trade, with no registration reqired.

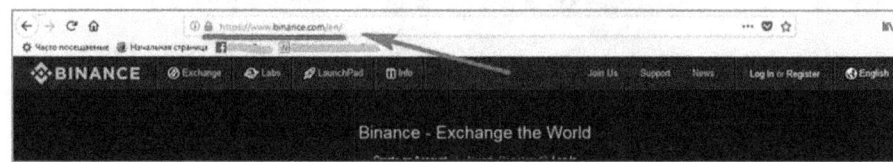

*Picture 1*

In the upper right corner, we find the "Register" button and click on it (Pic.2).

*Picture 2*

Then, you will see a new window (Pic. 3). It is simple. Enter your e-mail, enter the password, and repeat the password. If there is an affiliate link, we copy the link and paste it in, but it is not necessary. Put the tick "I agree to Binance's Terms of Use," and press the "Register" button.

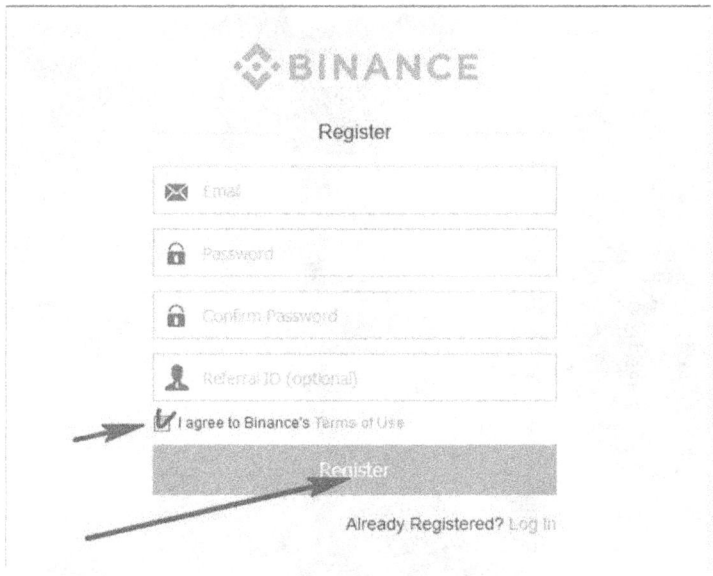

Picture 3

You will see a window with capcha (Pic.4). Binance uses a rather unusual captcha. Some users don't always understand what to do next. But in fact, everything is quite simple; you need to drag the slider 1 to the right until the puzzle 2 takes its place.

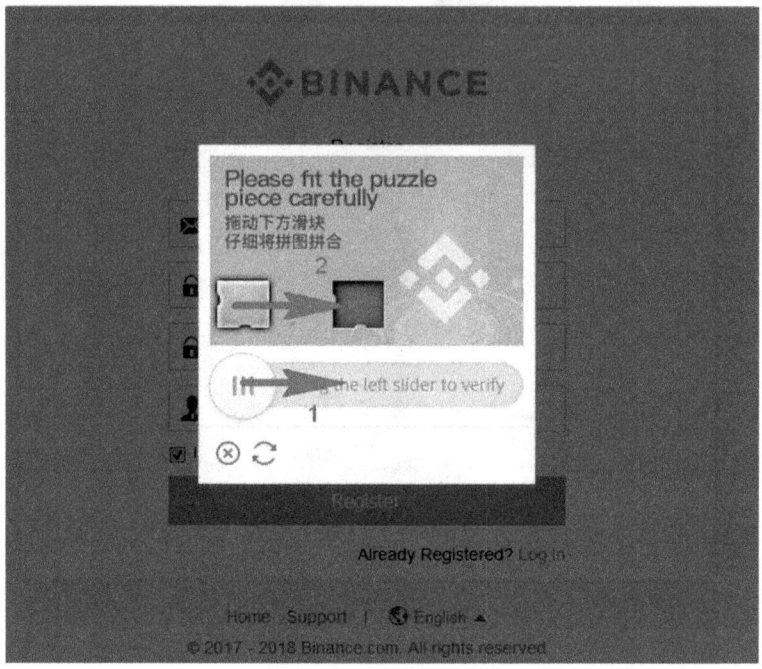

*Picture 4*

In the next window (Pic. 5), you are informed of a message that has been sent to your inbox in order to verify the authenticity of your e-mail. Go to your inbox and find there a letter from Binance.

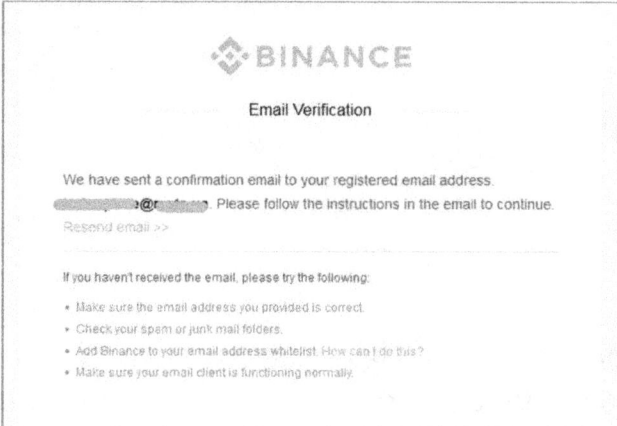

*Picture 5*

Open it and press "Verify Email," or copy the link and paste it into the address box of the browser (Pic. 6).

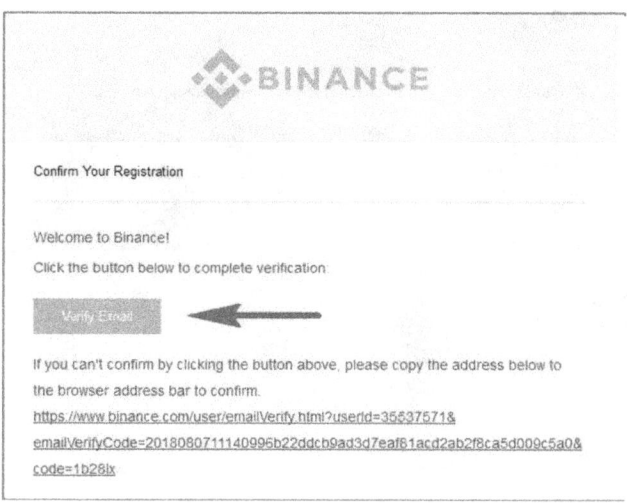

*Picture 6*

Congratulations! Your Binance account was successfully registered (Pic. 7).

*Picture 7*

Before you start trading, let's wait a little and look around for a while. Use your login and password to enter the exchange (Pic. 8).

*Picture 8*

Once you are there, a window appears with some security work recommendations (Pic. 9).

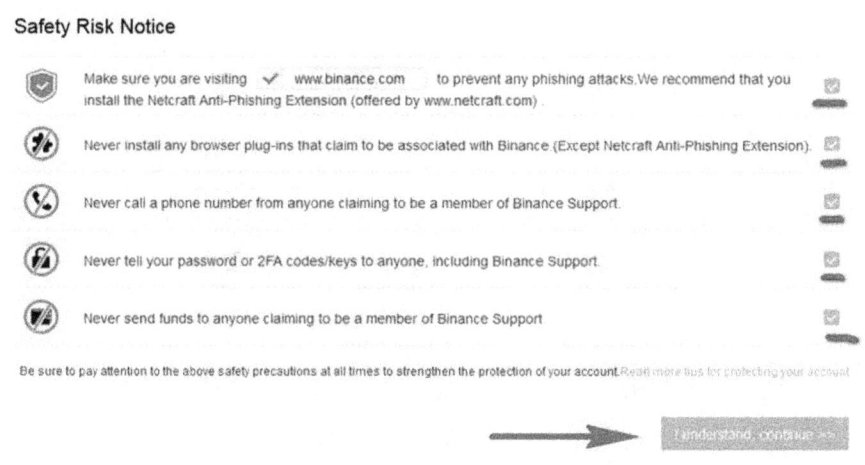

*Picture 9*

You're asked to check the address in the address box of the browser; don't install various ads on your browser, and don't tell anyone your phone number, which has been provided to the exchange for authentication. Don't tell anyone your password and secret code; remember that the exchange employees will never ask you to transfer any funds to them. You should agree with all of the points, put all of the checkmarks everywhere, and press the "I understand, continue" button.

At the last stage, you will be offered to go through a two-factor verification (Pic.10).

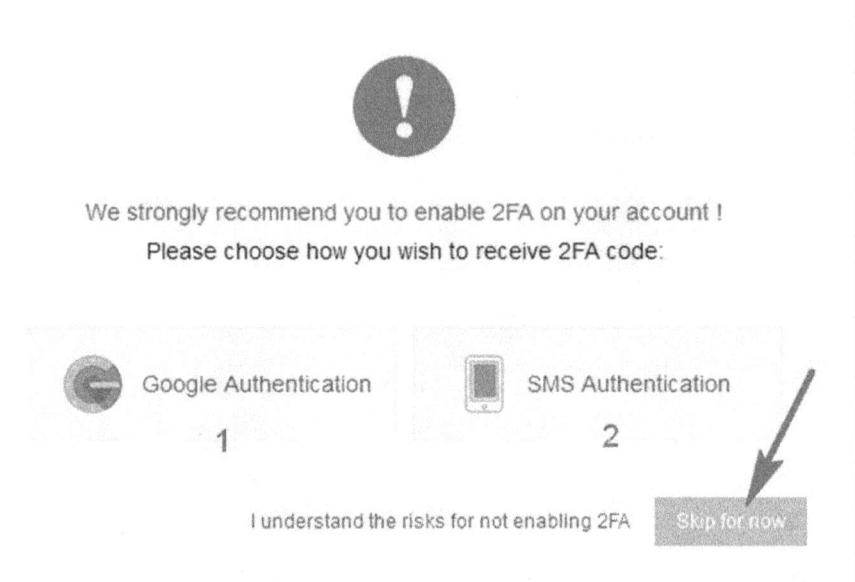

*Picture 10*

You can do this either through the Google app or via SMS. I recommend you go through this procedure later and skip this step for now by pressing the "Skip for now" button.

Well, you are on your Binance exchange account finally! Here, you will find: (Pic.11)

Picture 11

1. Your Email

2. Verification level – 1 diamond

3. You are offered to use the BNB exchange coin to pay the commission—this will reduce the commission by 25 percent. This feature is activated immediately. My advice to you, don't turn it off.

4. Further, you can see your level of verification again. It gives you the ability to withdraw not more than 2 BTC per day.

5. Two diamonds verification status gives you the ability to withdraw not more than 100 BTC per day. You need to provide your documents for verification in case you want to do it.

6. If you need to withdraw a larger amount, you will need three diamonds status and technical support.

Now, let us look at some of the paragraphs on the top menu, namely those which you'll need for work at the beginning (Pic. 12).

Picture 12

There are only two sub-paragraphs in the first paragraph of the exchange main menu:

1. «Basic» - is a simplified version of the exchange trading platform. It is not overloaded with tools and graphics. If it´s your first time on an exchange, start with it.

2. «Advanced» - Once the simplified interface becomes clear and familiar to you then easily move to more the complex presentation of the trading platform. Here, you'll find more graphs and tools to analyze.

We'll skip the next three main menu paragraphs, "Labs," "LaunchPad," and "Info," since you won´t need them at the beginning of your work. Let's pay attention to the paragraph "Funds" (Pic.13) and its submenu:

*Picture 13*

1. «Balances» - shows the balance of all coins that you have.

2. «Deposits» - Here, you'll find your deposits, when, how much, and what kind of coin you bring to the exchange.

3. «Withdrawals» - is the opposite of the previous one, which shows when, how much, and what coin you withdrew from the exchange.

4. «Transactions» - the last one in the submenu. Here, you'll be able to see all of the transactions in general and for each coin separately. Besides, you can download a complete or partial report on the movement of your funds for the specified period in an Excel spreadsheets format.

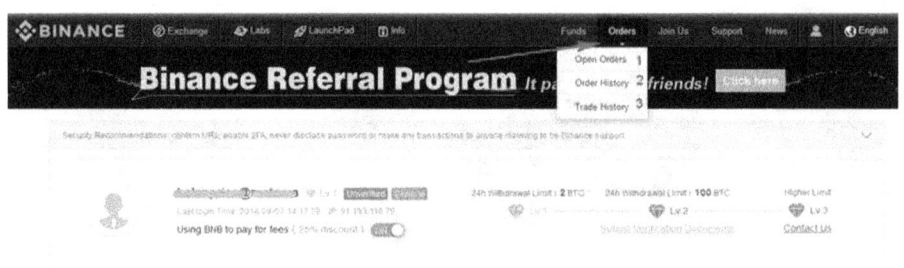

*Picture 14*

Other reports you'll be able to see are in the folowing (Pic. 14):

1. «Open orders» - all open orders for postponed purchase or sale of coins.

2. «Order history» - shows the history of postponed orders and the market ones (we'll talk about these orders in the next chapter).

3. «Trade history» - shows the history of your purchases and sales.

You can download the report in Excel format from each of these menu options.

In the penultimate paragraph of the menu, you will be able to see (Pic. 15):

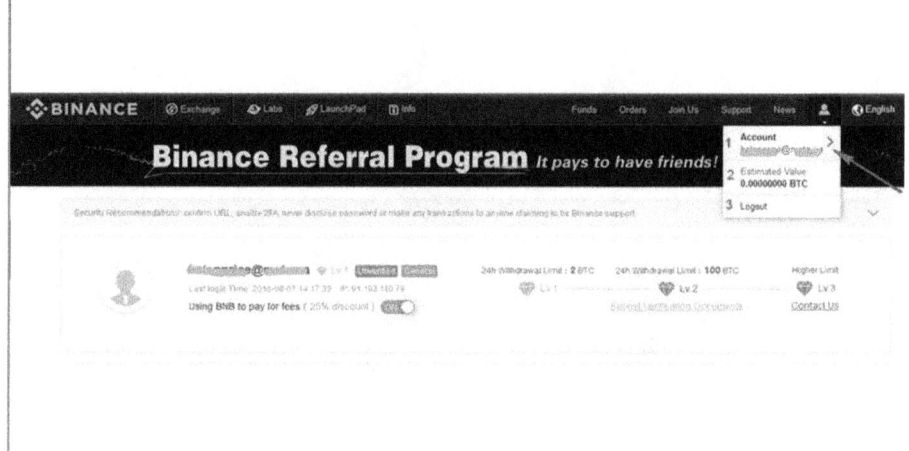

*Picture 15*

1. «Account» - view your account information, make changes, connect two-factor verification, and so on.

2. «Estimated Value» - shows your total balance at the exchange in bitcoins.

3. «Logout» - allows the user to exit the account.

Well, that is all for the beginning. Of course, work on the Binance exchange, as well as on any other one, requires more knowledge and skills, but that all comes with time and experience. And in order to gain the experience, you should start with the simplest exchange.

## CHAPTER 6
# First Binance Trade Steps

To start trading on the exchange, we need just a few steps:

- Bring money to the exchange
- Find out all about the orders

Let's start step by step. We´ll look of the balance refill on the exchange using the example of bitcoin. Log in to your account at Binance. Enter the "Deposits" menu.

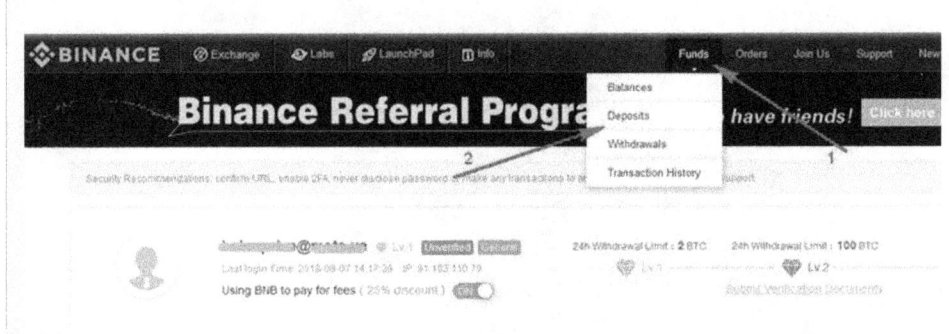

*Picture 16*

You will see a deposit refill window (Pic. 17).

Picture 17

Enter in the search box "BTC" and select the bitcoin. Now, you are able to see the number of your bitcoin wallet on the Binance exchange (Pic. 18).

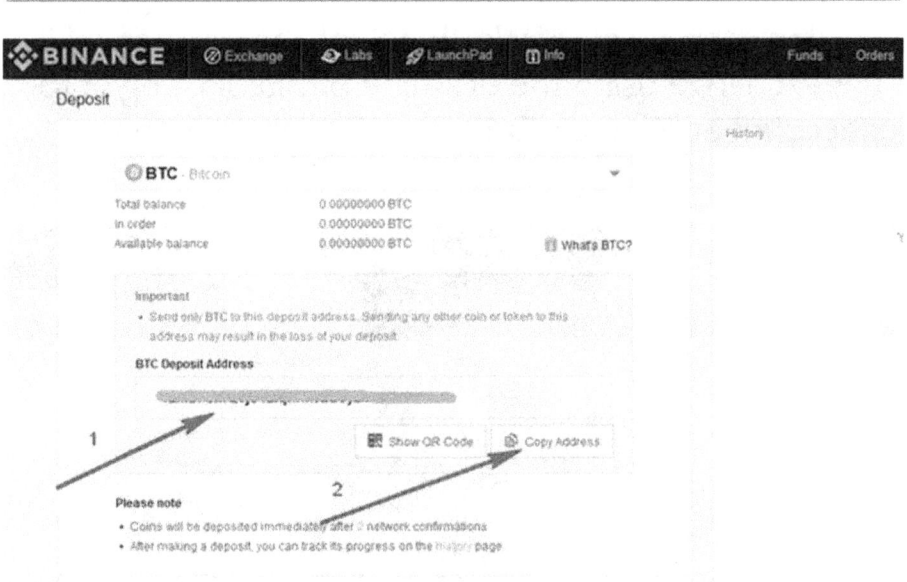

Picture 18

Purchase some bitcoins and transfer them to this account. The bitcoins can be bought on various exchanges or services, such as **Coinbase** (www.coinbase.com) or **Localbitcoin** (localbitcoins.com).

So, you should copy your Binance exchange bitcoin wallet address, then insert it in the Coinbase service (or any service for exchanging cryptocurrency) and wait until money arrives on the exchange balance. This can be checked on the "Deposits" or "Balances" tabs. Then, a list of all coins traded by the exchange would be shown.

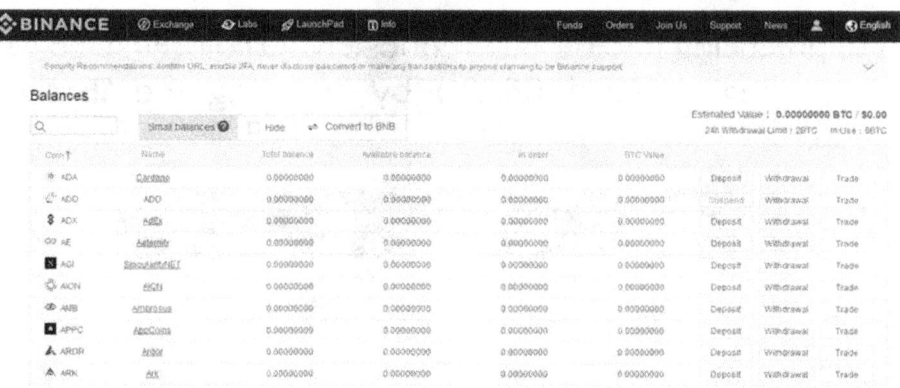

*Picture 19*

If money already is on your account, you'll be able to see it in several places at once (Pic.20).

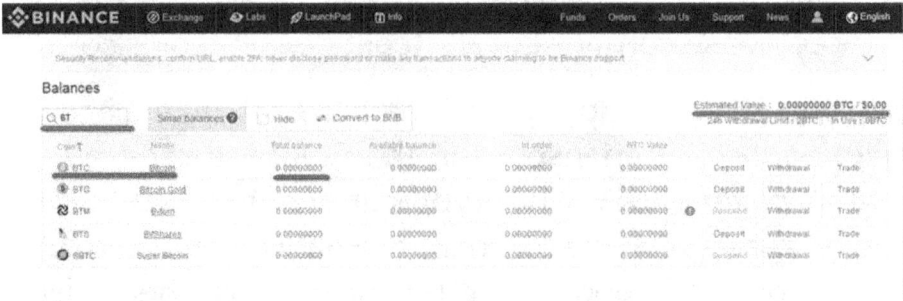

Picture 20

For practicing trading, let's choose NEO coin. First, go to the trading terminal (Pic.21) by selecting the "Basic" menu.

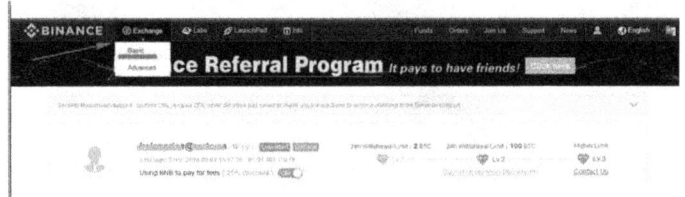

Picture 21

Select the "BTC" marker in the window to the right (Pic.22), then enter "NEO" in the search box, and select NEO coin paired with bitcoin.

Picture 22

Now, the information about this coin is in front of us (Pic. 23):

*Picture 23*

1. Its name
2. Price in bitcoin and USD
3. Price changing chart
4. One hour interval

By scrolling a page down, you´ll be able to see (Pic. 24):

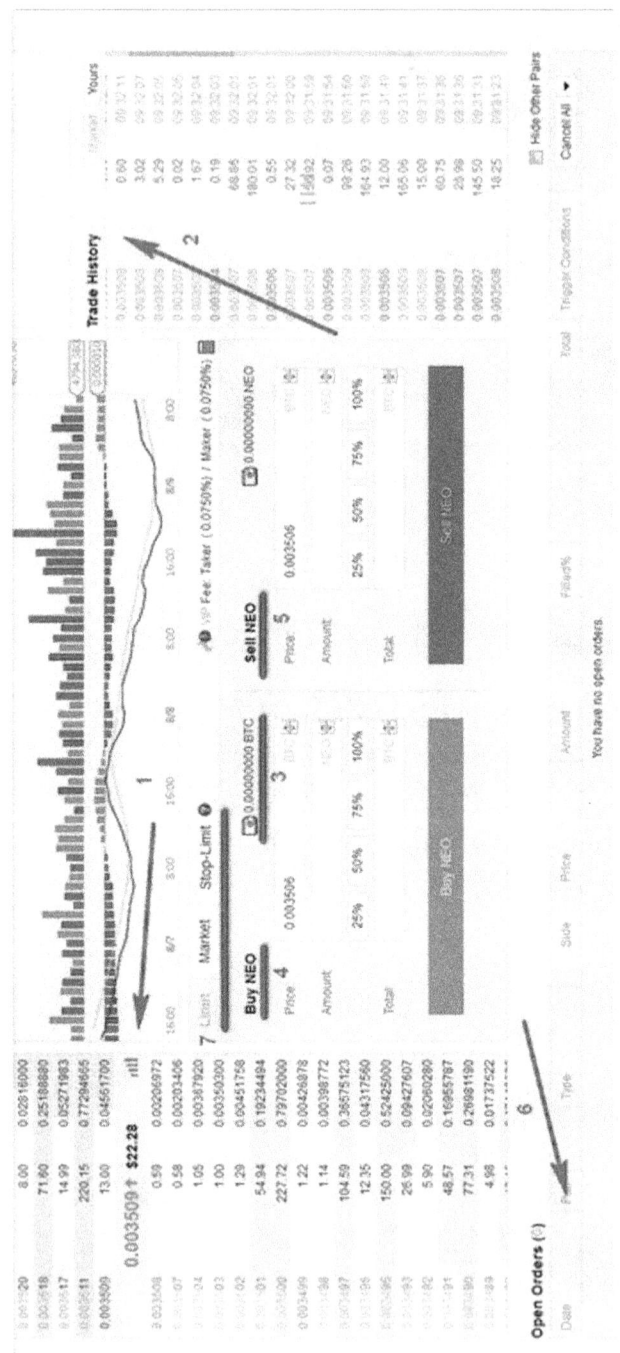

*Picture 24*

1. The order book is a list of pending orders for sale and purchase of coins on the exchange
2. The coin trade history
3. Bitcoin wallet balance
4. Purchase conditions
5. Sale conditions
6. The list of your orders for the purchase of coins, if there is any
7. The options to choose one of three orders for buying or selling coins

Before you buy or sell a coin, you need to figure out which order you want to buy it with.

**"Limit"** order assumes one condition: if the coin's price is equal to the specified value, then you´ll be able to buy a certain number of coins. For example, the Neo coin price at the moment is 0.003508 BTC; however, the chart shows even lower price a few hours ago— 0.003390 BTC. Thus, if we are interested in buying a coin at a lower price, we should set up the price we want; for example, 0.003445 BTC on the "Limit" tab on the "Price" line. Specify the desired number of coins you want to purchase (within the capabilities of your bitcoin-wallet), and press the BUY button. Your purchase order of coins goes to the order book of the exchange and also to your open list of orders (Pic. 24 paragraph 6). The coins are bought by the purchase order once the price of the coins falls to the specified price by you.

The **"Market"** tab lets you buy or sell a coin according to a market price; in our case, at a price of 0.003508 BTC. In this case, you no longer have the opportunity to set a price but only indicate the number of coins you are ready to buy or sell (Pic.25).

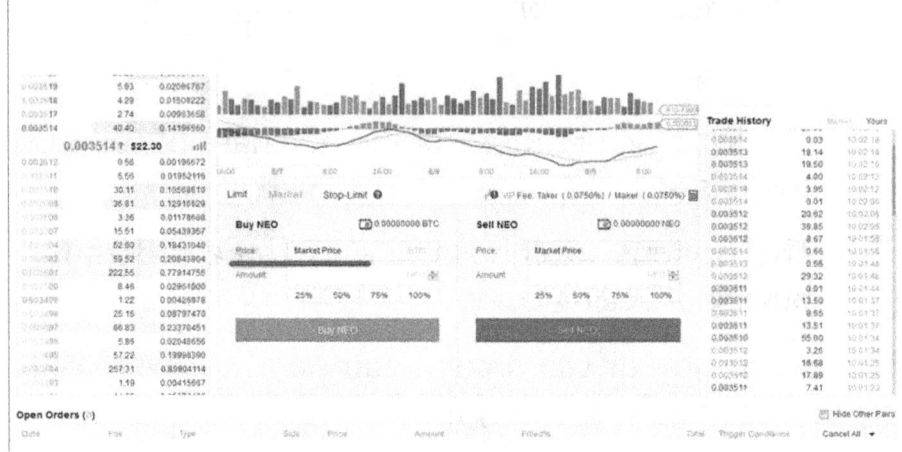

*Picture 25*

And the last tab "Stop-Limit" allows us to place an order with two conditions (Pic.26):

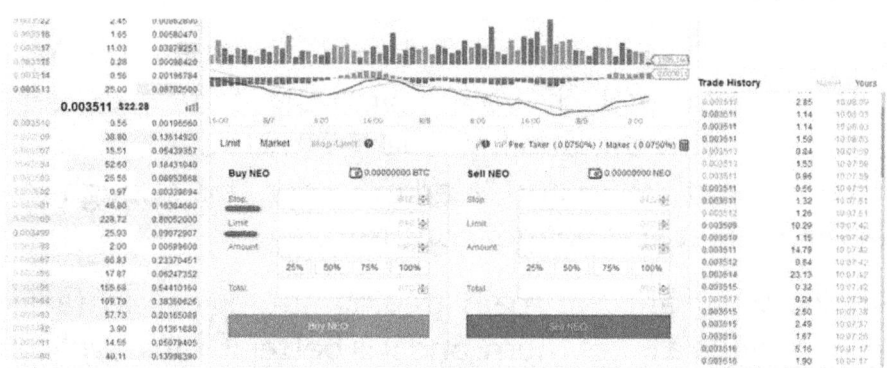

Picture 26

- The "Stop" line allows us to specify the price at which our order will be activated.
- The "Limit" line contains the price we are ready to pay for a deal.

Then we need to specify the number of coins and press the buy or sell button.

When the first condition—"Stop"—is activated, such an order appears in the book of orders. Let me give you an example. Supposedly, we want to buy a coin only if the price goes down. Therefore, we set the following condition: if the price of the coin falls to 0.003450 BTC, then we want our purchase order at the price of 0.003445 BTC to be placed. Once the price of NEO drops to the level of 0.003450 BTC, your order will appear in the book of orders, and if the price falls even lower, to 0.003445 BTC, your transaction will be completed.

**"Stop-Limit"** orders are applied for certain trading strategies; however, if you have just started to get acquainted with the stock exchange, then start trading with the "Limit" order and "Market" order. It is enough to feel the market and not get confused.

Finally, what are the main trading strategies? In fact, there are quite a lot of them, and it is better if you develop your own one day. Generally speaking, within a single exchange, you can trade in one of the following methods.

## Scalping

You buy a coin at one price and sell it at a price 3-5 percent higher. In order to earn here, you need to make up to one hundred transactions per day. This is a rather intense way of trading; however, it does not require a very deep analysis of the market. To start trading, you need to choose some number of coins with 5-10 percent volatility. Nonetheless, such a strategy requires your constant presence at the market.

## Daytrading

This method requires less stress, but you will need to analyze the coins more carefully.

The difference between buying and selling coins according to this method can vary from 5 to 15 percent. It takes a day or three if the market is active.

## Long Term Investments

With this approach, you can earn from 200 to 400 percent of your deposit! But it will take more time—at least six months. In this case, you won't need to sit at the monitor every day and watch the graphics. Select two to five coins then buy them. The next step is to distribut the deposit between them and wait until they grow in price in order to sell it with a good profit.

Of course, this all is oversimplified, but enough to try to understand if you want to go deeper with it.

## CHAPTER 7
# The Most Important

Finally, dear reader, I would like to talk about the most important factor.

With any business, investment is a very risky part. If we talk about trading on the exchange, then contrary to rumors, this is a hard but very exciting work. Here, you´ll experience not only ups but also falls. In order to not fail and not be disappointed, you should follow some simple but very important rules.

Trading on the exchange is primarily a psychology, a mentality. There is no place for emotions and passions; otherwise, you will lose everything. You need to learn patience, perseverance, and endurance. If you can´t handle your emotions, don´t consider further steps, because following them, you won't have enough self-restraint. Therefore, trading isn´t for you; thus, you could receive income from long-term investments.

You need to learn. As we mentioned above, you need to develop your own trading strategy. To gain the experience, it will take time. But the most important thing is a diary of trades! You need to keep a record of your transactions, constantly and carefully. Otherwise, you won't learn anything.

**Risk Management.** Beginner, starting trade on the exchange, asks himself a question: how much can I earn? This is a good question, but it is not in its place. First of all, you need to understand how much you can afford to lose. Yes, Yes! It is to lose. That's life! This is an exchange! You must learn how to control your risks and capital. Your first task on the stock exchange is not to lose your capital. Your second task is to multiply it. Only after that can you can think about getting a high profit.

**Never** take credit for trading on the exchange. Don´t take money from your family budget, such as training, insurance, etc. Allocate a small percentage (5-10 percent) of your budget, which you will regularly invest.

**Never stop learning** and keep in mind that you can learn to trade **only in practice**. Take a risk only with small capital without being afraid of losing it.

# CONCLUSION

I believe that cryptocurrency has already entered our life, as it was with fiat money. And sooner or later, we will all benefit from its advantages and suffer from disadvantages, as it happens with credit cards today. In any case, cryptocurrency deserves our attention, so make an opinion about it. This book is a brief introduction to the cryptocurrency trade world. If you decide to try, then be patient and perseverant, learn, and practice. I sincerely wish you success!

CPSIA information can be obtained
at www.ICGtesting.com
Printed in the USA
LVHW020824050721
691871LV00021B/1211